T0113881

GRADES **K-2**

INCLUSION
ACTIVITIES THAT WORK!

Toby J.
KARTEN

CORWIN PRESS
Classroom

Copyright © 2008 by Corwin Press

All rights reserved. When reproducible pages are included, their use is authorized for individuals, classroom use, and noncommercial entities who have purchased the book. Except for that usage, no part of this book may be reproduced or utilized in any form or by any means, electronic or mechanical, including photocopying, recording, or by any information storage and retrieval system, without permission in writing from the publisher.

For information:

Corwin Press
A SAGE Publications Company
2455 Teller Road
Thousand Oaks, California 91320
CorwinPress.com

SAGE Publications, Ltd.
1 Oliver's Yard
55 City Road
London EC1Y 1SP
United Kingdom

SAGE Publications India Pvt. Ltd.
B 1/I 1 Mohan Cooperative
Industrial Area
Mathura Road, New Delhi
India 110 044

SAGE Publications Asia-Pacific Pvt. Ltd.
33 Pekin Street #02-01
Far East Square
Singapore 048763

ISBN 978-1-4129-5233-0

This book is printed on acid-free paper.

08 09 10 11 12 10 9 8 7 6 5 4 3 2 1

Executive Editor: Kathleen Hex
Managing Developmental Editor: Christine Hood
Editorial Assistant: Anne O'Dell
Proofreader: Bette Darwin
Art Director: Anthony D. Paular
Cover Designer: Rose Storey
Cover and Interior Production Artist: Karine Hovsepian

INCLUSION
ACTIVITIES THAT WORK!

GRADES **K-2**

TABLE OF CONTENTS

Connections to Standards

This chart shows the national academic standards covered in each unit.

LANGUAGE ARTS	Standards are covered on pages
1	23, 37
2	23, 37
3	12, 13, 15, 17, 20, 23, 26
4	10, 15, 22, 26, 27, 29, 30
5	10, 20, 29, 31, 33
6	35, 37
8	10, 37
10	71
11	37
12	17

MATHEMATICS	Standards are covered on pages
Numbers and Operations 1	39, 42, 45, 49
Numbers and Operations 2	45, 49
Numbers and Operations 3	42, 45, 49
Algebra 1	39, 49
Algebra 3	39, 45
Geometry 1	53
Geometry 4	42, 53
Measurement 1	45, 53
Measurement 2	45, 53
Data Analysis and Probability 1	42, 56
Data Analysis and Probability 2	56
Data Analysis and Probability 3	17
Problem Solving 1	45, 49

Communication 1	39, 45
Communication 2	39, 45, 53
Communication 4	42
Connections 1	12, 39, 45, 53, 54
Representation 1	39, 42, 45, 49, 53
Representation 2	49
Representation 3	53

SOCIAL STUDIES	Standards are covered on pages
Understand the ways human beings view themselves in and over time	58, 66, 68, 76, 83, 85, 87
Understand individual development and identity	66, 69
Understand interactions among individuals, groups, and institutions	71

Introduction

Educators teaching students with exceptionalities in general education classrooms need practical tools and strategies to help ease their workloads, while meeting individual needs and standards at the same time. As difficult as it may sound, it is indeed possible to simultaneously embrace standards and differences, differences in abilities, learning styles, and intelligences. With the right tools, appropriate accommodations and modifications can be seamlessly and appropriately applied.

This book attempts to ease frustrations and replace them with proactive, research-based, effective strategies that apply across the curriculum. A multitude of activities offer practical ways to embrace educational standards, while differentiating the learning. These activities are not intended to replace your curriculum. Instead, they are designed to enhance your instructional repertoire through active learning environments that accommodate students' differing needs.

As an educator, you know your students best. The activities in this book can be adapted or modified to meet the needs of specific students in your classroom. In addition, this book includes teacher-friendly inclusion forms designed to simplify the inclusion process. Use them to help with documentation, communication, reflection, organization, and inclusion implementation. These forms help break through the educational jargon to provide direct, simple support.

As educators, meeting the standards is not the goal; *exceeding* the standards is the goal! Instead of thinking "My students can't do this," change your thought process to "*How* can I get them to do this?" Concentrate on strengths, not weaknesses. The eighteen activities are the backbone of the lessons offered in this book (see page 7). These approaches can be applied to a student with vision or hearing impairment, a student who has high cognitive needs, a student with behavioral challenges, as well as a student with more advanced skills. This book provides the "roadmap" to inspire the potentials and strengths of all learners and educators. Enjoy the journey!

Valuable Everyday Activities to Promote Inclusion

- Establish prior knowledge.

- Preplan lessons with structured objectives, allowing for inter- and post-planning.

- Proceed from the simple to the complex by using discrete task analysis, which breaks up learning into its parts, while still valuing the whole.

- Use a step-by-step approach, teaching in small bites, with lots of practice and repetition for those who need it.

- Reinforce abstract concepts with concrete examples.

- Think about possible accommodations and modifications that might be needed.

- Incorporate sensory elements including visual, auditory, and kinesthetic/tactile.

- Teach to students' strengths to help compensate for their weaknesses.

- Concentrate on individual students, not syndromes.

- Provide opportunities for success to build self-esteem.

- Give positives before negatives.

- Use modeling with both teachers and peers.

- Vary types of instruction and assessment, with multiple intelligences and cooperative learning.

- Make learning relevant by relating it to students' lives using interest inventories.

- Remember the basics, proper hygiene, respecting others, and effective listening, in addition to the "three R's": reading, writing, and arithmetic.

- Establish a pleasant classroom environment that encourages students to ask questions and become actively involved in their learning.

- Increase students' self-awareness of levels and progress.

- Provide many opportunities to effectively communicate and collaborate with parents, students, and colleagues.

Put It into Practice

Special education is at a crossroads—crossroads that have been repaved and redirected again and again. Why can't we just get it right? The answer is that perhaps there is no "universal right." We strive for universal rights in our world, yet differing political, economic, social, spiritual, and in this case, educational thoughts and policies abound. Academia conducts research, studies are carried out, and theories about best practices are born. The ultimate goal is to transfer the research into immediate practical benefits for students in that laboratory called the classroom.

The dilemma is that we live in a diverse world, one in which people have differing needs and abilities. Consequently, how could these theories then be universal? Is there such a thing as a universal lesson that meets the needs of all students? Can a student with severe cognitive impairments benefit from the same strategies as a student with more advanced skills? It is a challenge we all face in today's inclusive classrooms.

Instructional strategies are only beneficial when they match students' diverse needs. Administrators, educators, parents, and even students can become frustrated by the ever-changing legislative demands that although designed to benefit those with special needs, often create schisms among personnel at school, caregivers at home, and students themselves. Professionals need to both apply and raise curriculum standards making sure everyone is on the same page. The purpose here is to erase frustrations and replace them with research-based, effective strategies that apply across the curriculum, and that embrace school and home environments, and the potentials and strengths of all learners (Odom, Brantlinger, Gersten, Horner, Thompson, & Harris, 2005).

For example, students who have phonemic awareness skills are likely to have an easier time learning to read and spell than students who have few or none of these skills (Armbruster & Osborn, 2001). The National Council for Teachers of Mathematics says that students in grades K–2 must have standards that help them understand numbers, ways of representing numbers, relationships among numbers, and number systems. Do these standards apply for all or just some learners? Now that inclusion is the thrust, educators are compelled and driven to find ways to deliver the same standards to students of differing abilities. This needs to begin at these crucial early grades.

Educators can effectively instruct students of all abilities and potentials, having high regard for all, while embracing individuality.

Professionals can design lessons that include students with exceptionalities, such as those with diverse physical, behavioral, social, learning, and cognitive levels. The standards in general education must be accessible to those students with the most and least needs, and everyone in between! Classrooms must create a healthy environment that both recognizes and nurtures students' strengths, so they can flourish into critical thinkers, ready to tackle the many challenges in their academic future.

Students are assessed on the knowledge they gain. Schools are required to meet Adequate Yearly Progress (AYP) under No Child Left Behind (NCLB), with the Individuals with Disabilities Education Act (IDEA) still in place (Yell, Katsiyanna, & Shiner, 2006). Before alternate assessments are given, educators must look at the general education curriculum requirements and then make some decisions.

In the past, many learners with exceptionalities were often deleted from mainstream learning and placed in separate classes with lower requirements (Walsh & Conner, 2004). Unfortunately, this mindset then resulted in an adult population ill prepared to meet societal demands in the workforce and in social relationships. Today, special and general educators must collaborate to figure out ways that all students can and will be successful in school by creating and instilling high expectations, beginning with the early, formative grades.

Effective research studies and literature, with reference to specific instructional strategies, reveal the need for change (Harriott, 2004; Karten, 2005; McTighe, Seif, & Wiggins, 2004; Nolet & McLaughlin, 2005; Zull, 2004). Educators in the field are arduously trying to include students with special needs in general education classrooms. In this effort, researchers, administrators, parents, students, and teachers can all play on the same team. Delivering knowledge through principles such as step-by-step-learning while accommodating for individual differences and strengths results in strategic, meaningful, applicable, and long-lasting learning for all!

CHAPTER 1

Reading

Words open up the world to children, one letter at a time. Systematic, research-based reading instruction beginning at an early age helps students to comprehend written words and the sounds they represent, unlocking a vast world of knowledge!

Class Telephone Book

One way to introduce nonfiction is to have students provide information about very important real people—themselves! This initial reading activity introduces students to a purpose for reading, specifically, finding information. Note: Before completing this activity, make sure to obtain parental permission for sharing personal information.

1. Give students a copy of the **Class Telephone Book reproducible (page 11)**. Help them fill out the personal information, including name, address, and telephone number. At the bottom of the page, invite each student to draw a picture of him- or herself.

Inclusion Tip

If students do not like drawing or have less developed fine motor skills, they can attach a photograph, an illustration from a magazine, or computer clip art.

2. As a class, help students alphabetize all the last names. Emphasize that names in a telephone book are organized in alphabetical order by last names.

3. Copy the pages to make a class telephone book for each student. Bind the pages together with a construction paper cover and have students decorate it.

4. Distribute a book to each student in the class. Invite students to illustrate the covers and title the book, for example: *Ms. Heidi Helpful's 1st Grade Class Telephone Book*.

5. Invite student pairs to "read for information." Ask them questions such as: *On what street does Ava Brooks live?*

6. Extend the activity by helping students practice making phone calls, memorizing their home phone numbers and addresses, or looking through a community directory.

Class Telephone Book

Directions: Fill in the page.

_____

- -

My Name: _____

My Address:

_____

- -

_____

_____

My Birthday:

_____

- -

_____

My Phone Number:

_____

- - - - - - - - - - - - - - - - - -

_____

Here is a picture of me!

Sounding Out Syllables

Young learners often need help sounding out multisyllabic words, syllable by syllable, to break the phonetic code. Big words are less intimidating when they are broken down and read one part at a time. This activity helps students pronounce syllables separately and place them in the correct order to form words.

1. Copy the syllables of several words on separate index cards, for example, *com-mu-ni-ty*.

2. Tell students that these syllables make up one word. They should sound out each syllable and then put the syllables in the correct order to form the word. They can also refer to the numbers.

3. After students put syllables in the correct order, have them write the whole word on a piece of paper and read it aloud.

4. Continue with several other words, encouraging students to sound out each syllable before putting them in order.

Inclusion Tip

Other ways students can learn letters and word parts kinesthetically include "writing" letters or syllables in the air or in a tray of salt or sand. Students can also clap their hands or tap their feet to syllables.

Sound Search

This activity helps students identify where they hear specific sounds in words. You can use it on an ongoing basis for targeting one or more consonants or consonant digraphs each day. Review sounds from the previous lesson to reinforce learning, or introduce new sounds.

1. Ahead of time, develop a word list that focuses on consonant or vowel sounds at the beginning, middle, and end of the words. For example:

B	C	D	F
because	**c**ould	**d**ear	**f**ish
a**b**ove	po**ck**et	a**dd**ition	a**f**ter
gra**b**	so**ck**	see**d**	stu**ff**

2. Make several copies of the **Sound Search reproducible (page 14)** for each student.

3. Tell students you are going to choose a target letter sound. Then you are going to read aloud a list of words. For each word, students will identify whether they hear the target sound at the beginning, middle, or end of the word. Remind students to think about where they hear the sound, not how the word might be spelled.

4. On their reproducibles, have students circle *B* for *beginning*, *M* for *middle*, or *E* for *end* to indicate where in the word they heard the target sound.

5. Continue reading words from your list until students have a good grasp of the concept. Repeat this activity throughout the year to reinforce learning.

Inclusion Tips

Use this concrete activity to help learners with language differences and those with lesser prior vocabulary knowledge.

If some students have auditory processing difficulties or hearing disabilities, you can pantomime meanings, and/or hold up pictures or classroom objects with these sounds so students have visuals to accompany spoken words.

Sound Search

Directions: Where do you hear the sound? Circle B for beginning, M for middle, or E for end.

1. B   M   E

2. B   M   E

3. B   M   E

4. B   M   E

5. B   M   E

6. B   M   E

7. B   M   E

8. B   M   E

Words in Words

There are many ways students can figure out how to pronounce words, such as breaking up words into syllables, sounds, or word parts. Increasing awareness of how words are formed allows learners to transfer decoding skills to their reading. Large words can be intimidating to young learners. Breaking down compound words allows students to recognize smaller, readable parts. It also helps them with comprehension. For example, reading and understanding the word doghouse is easier when you separate the words dog and house. What is a doghouse? A house for a dog!

Use the Words in Words reproducible (page 16) to help students find smaller words inside larger words, or compound words. Ask them to write the words separately, and then together again to form the whole word.

After students complete the practice sheet, generate a similar chart on a computer titled My Compound Words List. Give each student several copies. As they read, students can record compound words they find in their chart. Invite students to keep their charts in their reading folder.

Inclusion Tip

To help concrete learners, write the two parts of each compound word on separate index cards and direct students to rearrange each pair of cards. The activity now has a self-correcting component. For example, a *flybutter* just doesn't fly, but a *butterfly* would!

Name _____   Date _____

Words in Words

Directions: Write the two words that make up each compound word.

Picture of Word	Compound Word	Word 1	Word 2	Write the Compound Word
	goldfish			
	doghouse			
	butterfly			
	cupcake			

Reading for Meaning

While students can often recognize words when reading, they may attach little meaning to those words. Using pictures helps students make the connection between words and meaning. It is also a great way to build students' vocabularies.

To reinforce this concept, give students a copy of the **Taking Care of Myself reproducible (page 18)**. Students will circle a word or picture to correctly complete each sentence. In doing so, they will make that valuable connection between words and pictures to create meaning.

Inclusion Tip

Students with less background knowledge or differing auditory, learning, and cognitive levels appreciate this type of activity. It complements their visual strengths!

Cause and Effect

Cause and effect is an inferential reading competency that goes beyond gathering information. It is a skill that requires students to apply, manipulate, and evaluate information. Students learn to see relationships between ideas.

Give students a copy of the **Cause and Effect reproducible (page 19)**. Help them read the text and pictures. Initiate a discussion about the cause–effect relationship in each scene. Then ask students to complete these cause–effect statements:

1. If you do not set your alarm, then . . .

2. If you do not brush your teeth, then . . .

3. If you are not dressed for the weather, then . . .

4. If you do not eat breakfast, then . . .

5. If you forget your homework, then . . .

6. If you are late to the bus stop, then . . .

7. If you are grumpy in school, then . . .

8. If you do not listen to your teacher, then . . .

9. If you do not try hard in school, then . . .

Name _____ Date _____

Taking Care of Myself

Directions: Circle the correct word or picture to finish each sentence.

1. I use a  to brush my teeth.

2. I use my  to fix my hair.

3. When I sneeze, I must use a .

4. If I cough, I must cover my  .

5. I must wash my 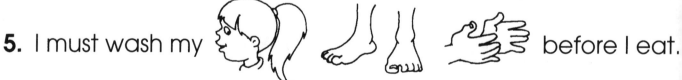 before I eat.

6. I always wear a     when I ride my bike.

Cause and Effect

Directions: Read and look at the picture in each box.

1. I wake up in the morning because I set my alarm clock.	**2.** I brush my teeth and wash my face to keep clean and healthy. 	**3.** I check the weather to decide what clothes to wear. 
4. I eat a good breakfast so I have energy for my day. 	**5.** I bring my homework to school so I will be ready for class. 	**6.** I get to the bus stop early so I don't miss my ride to school.
7. I am nice and polite to my classmates. 	**8.** I listen to my teacher so I am ready to follow the day's schedule. 	**9.** I raise my hand and ask questions so I can learn. 

Word Families

Learning words in groups, or families, is a great way to improve students' vocabulary and spelling skills. This activity appeals to the multiple intelligences: visual-spatial, verbal-linguistic, bodily-kinesthetic, and interpersonal.

Give students a copy of the **Word Families reproducible (page 21)**. Encourage them to draw pictures or write words in the boxes for each word family. Invite students to list additional words on the back if they can.

Extend the Activity

After students complete the activity, invite them to take turns acting out some of the words in small groups. Tell them to say the word family first, such as: *My word is in the −et family.* The student then pretends to fly like a jet until classmates guess the word *jet!*

Sample Word Families List

at: bat, cat, fat, hat, mat, pat, rat, sat, flat, that
et: jet, let, met, net, pet, set, wet, yet
ip: dip, hip, lip, nip, rip, sip, tip, zip, chip, clip, drip, flip, grip, ship,
ot: cot, dot, hot, lot, not, pot, plot, shot, slot, spot, trot
ut: but, cut, gut, hut, jut, nut, rut, shut, strut

Inclusion Tip

Students with lower reading skills can look at the word lists or work in pairs. Students who are more advanced can list their own words.

Name _____   Date _____

Word Families

Directions: Write different letters in front of each letter pair. What new words can you make? Write new words or draw pictures in the boxes.

_____ at

_____ et

_____ ip

_____ ot

_____ ut

Manipulating Letters

Students learn more about words and their phonemes by manipulating and rearranging letters. This is a better alternative to repeatedly correcting misspelled or mispronounced words by erasing and rereading errors. Instead, in this activity, students move around letters until they find the correct "formula."

For this activity students will need a set of letter cards or a set of foam, wooden, or magnetic letter manipulatives. Give each student or pair of students a set of letter manipulatives. Tell them you are going to read aloud several words. For each word, they will arrange their letters to form the words. Encourage students to experiment with inserting or taking out different letters until they think they have letters arranged correctly to make the word.

Example Weekly Dictation

Day 1: cat, cap, cape, pace, tap, tape, pat, eat, tea, ate

Day 2: bet, beat, tab, bat, bats, sat, set, seat

Day 3: we, wet, went, west, sew, stew, new, nest

Day 4: lip, lap, pile, pal, pale, lie, pie, slip, pile, piles, pies, please

Day 5: pot, pout, top, stop, post, spot, up

Inclusion Tip

To add an additional tactile element, students using magnetic letters can rearrange the letters on a metal cookie sheet. Those using foam letters can float the letters in pie pans filled with water.

Extend the Activity

- Mix up a specific group of letters and ask students to arrange them in alphabetical order.

- Conduct a classroom sound search! Assign a different letter to each student. Then have students find objects in the classroom with those initial, medial, or final sounds in their names.

- Give students index cards with selected sight words or weekly vocabulary words written on them. Ask students to spell each word using letter manipulatives.

Story Stuffers

It's easier for students to make sense of a story if they can break it into parts. **The Story Stuffer graphic organizer (page 24)** will be one of students' favorite reading tools! Make several copies for each student. Every time students read a story, they can "stuff" their ideas about it into the organizer. Students can write words, phrases, simple sentences, or page numbers where the information can be found. Story organizers help students break down stories into elements such as beginning, middle, and end; plot; characters; and setting. They can also draw pictures to express their ideas.

Inclusion Tip

Reading buddies can work together to record story information. Then the class can work as a group to "stuff" story information into large manila envelopes labeled *characters, setting, events,* and *ending.*

The "Ws" of Reading Comprehension

Basic questions such as who, what, when, where, why, and how are key to helping students understand what they read. After reading a story individually or as a class, students can use the **Story Web graphic organizer (page 25)** to categorize and organize story details. You may want to ask students specific questions to prompt responses, such as those shown below.

Sample Questions

1. Who gave Cara the puppy?
2. Why did Cara get the puppy?
3. What is the puppy's name?
4. When did Cara tell the class about her puppy?
5. How does Cara feel?

Inclusion Tip

Prepare answer sheets for students with developing writing skills. When you ask a question, they can simply write the number to the question next to the appropriate answer.

Story Stuffer

Directions: In the boxes, write or draw pictures about a story you read.

Who?
People or Animals

Where? Place
When? Time

Plot
What Happened?

Ending
Tell about the last part.

Story Web

Directions: In the boxes, write about a story you read.

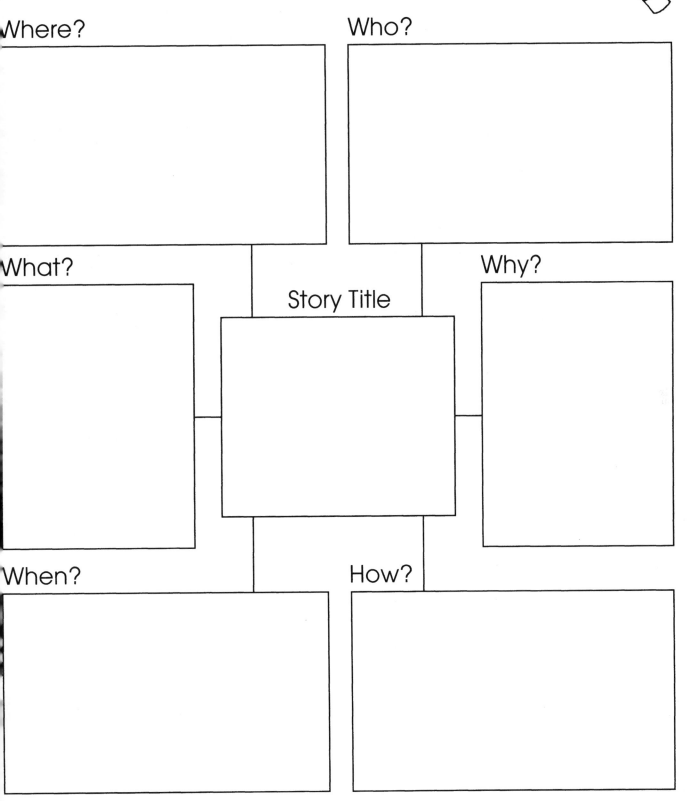

Where?

Who?

What?

Story Title

Why?

When?

How?

Listen and Learn

In this reading and listening activity, students follow along as you read a story aloud. All learners can benefit from listening to pauses, inflections, and letter sounds to gain better fluency. Ahead of time, prepare answer grids like the one below. To answer the questions, students write the corresponding question number inside the word box that shows the answer. Visual learners can read a copy of the words, while auditory learners listen to them.

Inclusion Tip

This type of oral reading activity is especially helpful for students with higher oral comprehension and lower word decoding skills. It also minimizes writing requirements for students with developing fine motor skills.

Example Story

Manuel slipped and slid his way to the school bus stop. The ground was covered with snow. He wore a warm sweater, boots, a hat, a coat, and gloves to stay warm. Even so, Manuel wished summer were here!

Sample Questions

1. What season is it?
2. What is on the ground?
3. What is Manuel wearing on his feet?
4. What keeps Manuel's hands warm?
5. What color is the ground?
6. To where is Manuel walking?
7. Did Manuel's mom drive him to school?
8. Name the season Manuel likes better.

Sample Answer Grid

gloves	boots	yes
bus stop	snow	no
white	winter	summer

Writing

From an early age, most students are fearful of writing their thoughts on paper. The first things they usually see are marks and corrections. Students must understand that writing is a form of communication that they can be edit, revise, and improve. They can write about anything they wish—their thoughts, ideas, stories, poems, letters, journals, and more!

Tell More About It

Before students become proficient writers, they must understand basic sentence structure and learn to identify and use the parts of speech, such as nouns, verbs, and adjectives. However, before using these terms, students can develop basic writing and describing skills using this simple, step-by-step approach.

1. Give students a copy of the **Tell More About It reproducible (page 28)**. They will learn how to use words to construct simple sentences.

2. Have students read each word on their reproducible, such as *kitten*.

3. Then have them write one describing word telling what the person or thing looks like, such as *fluffy, small,* or *striped*.

4. Ask them to write one action word describing something the person or thing does, such as *plays, sleeps,* or *purrs*.

5. Finally, have students use their words to write a simple sentence about the person or thing, such as *The fluffy kitten plays.*

Inclusion Tip

If students do not like drawing or have less-developed fine motor skills, they can attach a photograph, an illustration from a magazine, or computer clip art.

Tell More About It

Directions: Read the word. Write one word to describe this person or thing. Then write one word telling what this person or thing does.

People and Things	What Does It Look Like?	What Does It Do?
kitten	fluffy	plays
tree		
fish		

Directions: Write a sentence using your new words.

1. The fluffy kitten plays.

_____

2. _____

_____

3. _____

Word Shuffle

This activity helps to teach left-to-right progression and building sentences by adding or deleting words. This activity works especially well for kinesthetic learners.

Write groups of words and punctuation marks on different colored index cards (e.g., nouns, yellow; verbs, green; adjectives, blue). Tell students that nouns are yellow, verbs are green, and adjectives are blue. Explain that a sentence is a complete thought and it must contain a noun (person, place, or thing) and a verb (action word).

Place several word cards in the pocket chart, for example: *I, like, pizza, do, you.* Arrange the words into a sentence, for example: *I like pizza.* Then invite students to rearrange and insert new word cards to create a new sentence. For example: *Do you like pizza?* or *I do like pizza.* (Sticky notes work well too!) As students build sentences in the chart, have the rest of the class copy the sentences on paper at their desks. Note: When creating word cards, make several *The, A, An, I, We, He, She,* and *They* cards to use for beginning sentences. This reinforces the idea that sentences begin with a capital letter.

Inclusion Tip

To add a tactile element and reinforce letter-writing skills, write words with puffy paint or colored glue. Words will "jump off" the cards, and students can easily trace the letters with their fingers.

Sample Science Sentences

1. A rock is a solid.
2. Is a rock a solid?
3. Water is a liquid.
4. Is water a liquid?
5. Water is also a solid.
6. Is a rock a liquid?
7. Is water a solid?

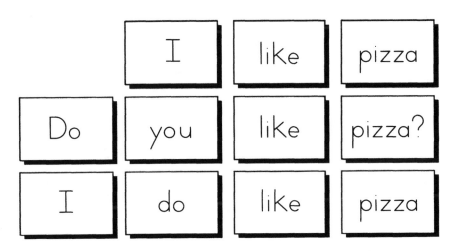

From A to Z

This alphabet activity helps students organize their thoughts and ideas before writing. Use the A to Z letter cards to help students associate letters with words and pictures. Give each student a set of 26 index cards. Ask them to write one letter of the alphabet in the top left corner of each card (you can do this prior to distribution if necessary). Invite students to write words, draw pictures, or glue magazine cutouts that begin with the matching letter. For example: *car* for *C*, *firefighter* for *F*, *house* for *H*, and *school* for *S*. Place a single hole punch in one corner of each card. Attach the card with a metal ring or string.

This activity can also be used to reinforce alphabetical order, initial sounds and letter correspondence, and left-to-right reading progression for early learners.

Inclusion Tip

Students who struggle with phonetic skills may need a "letter jump-start." Make a set of alphabetized shoeboxes or large envelopes containing pictures from which students can choose. Visual dictionaries help, too!

Words for the Five Senses

Descriptive writing is more vivid and interesting if students refer to what they see, hear, smell, touch, and taste. Words that appeal to the senses paint a more detailed picture for the reader.

Give students a copy of the **Words for the Five Senses reproducible (page 32)**. Invite students to suggest a place to describe (e.g., *beach, park, museum, school, carnival, zoo*). Ask them to think about what they might hear, see, smell, touch, and taste in that place. Then have students write descriptive words about the place under the correct headings.

After students have listed several describing words in their charts, ask them to write or dictate simple sentences using the following frame: *When I am at the _____, I can _____.* For example: *When I am at the park, I can smell flowers.*

Inclusion Tip

Keep a classroom sensory box containing concrete objects such as a lemon, cookie, brush, and cotton ball to elicit descriptive words such as *sour, sweet, prickly,* and *fluffy*.

Words for the Five Senses

Directions: Write words or draw pictures for the five senses.

Taste				
Touch				
Smell				
Hear				
See				

Steps to Good Writing

Young writers need guidance in their introduction to the writing process. Make sure students understand that good writing begins with a rough draft that is then revised and edited. Give students a copy of the **Make It Better reproducible (page 34).** This step-by-step approach guides students toward improving their writing skills. As they get older, they can start asking themselves these types of questions.

Inclusion Tip

To add kinesthetic and visual elements, invite student groups to form sentence teams who "wear" words on sticky notes. They can add, delete, or move sticky notes to form new sentences.

Configuration Boxes

Handwriting is a skill that is developed and perfected with repeated practice. Configuration boxes can help students "choreograph" their writing by placing letters in assigned spaces, or by drawing spaces around prewritten words to increase awareness of letter size and alignment. For example:

Write three simple words on large index cards. Place the word cards in a pocket chart. Then place another index card with configuration boxes matching one of the three words in the pocket chart. Invite students to guess which word goes in the boxes.

Invite a volunteer to the pocket chart to write the correct word in the configuration boxes. Repeat this activity using different word cards and configuration boxes, giving each student a chance to write.

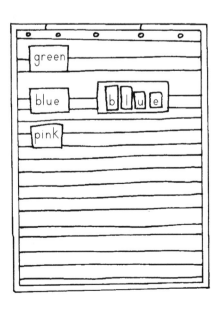

Inclusion Tip

To improve fine motor and visual perception skills, students can trace boxed letters or form letters from pipe cleaners.

Make It Better

Directions: Read each sentence. Then answer the questions. Write a better sentence.

Example:

I saw a bird.
What color was the bird? blue
When did you see the bird? after school
Where did you see the bird? in a tree
New sentence: I saw a blue bird in a tree after school

1. We went to the store.

_____
_____

2. What kind of store? _____

_____
_____

3. When did you go to the store? _____

_____
_____

4. Why did you go to the store? _____

_____
_____

5. New sentence: _____

Hurray for Homophones!

Homophones are words that sound alike but have different meanings and spellings. These kinds of words can be especially challenging for young students as they learn to read, write, and spell. Practice with homophones helps students develop their vocabularies and improve spelling skills.

Give students a copy of the **Hurray for Homophones! reproducible (page 36)**. Direct them to circle the word that correctly completes each sentence.

Then invite students to write a simple paragraph about the beach using their new sentences. Use this as an opportunity to model proper indentation to begin a paragraph, capitalization for the first word of a sentence, and ending punctuation. Encourage more advanced students to add new, interesting words and details to improve their sentences. Have students illustrate their paragraphs to share with the class.

Inclusion Tip

Show students how to use a beginner's dictionary. Keep picture dictionaries along with electronic spell checkers accessible in a reading station so students can verify their responses, meriting self-directed learning.

Extend the Activity

- Make flashcards with a homophone written on each side. Say a sentence aloud and ask students to hold up the correct spelling for the word.

- Write a homophone on the board, such as *sent*. Tell students the meaning of the word. Then ask them to tell you a homophone for that word. Challenge them to spell it and tell its meaning (e.g, *cent, scent*).

Hurray for Homophones!

Directions: Circle the word that correctly fits in each sentence.

1. The _____ is shining bright. (sun, son)

2. The sky is clear _____. (blue, blew)

3. I _____ pink shells in the sand. (see, sea)

4. Do you _____ the waves crashing? (here, hear)

5. The ocean feels warm on my _____. (feet, feat)

6. Let's swim _____ a while. (four, for)

7. Let's go to the beach next _____ too! (week, weak)

Capitals for the Capitals

This purposeful writing activity is not just a lesson in capitalization; it is also a lesson in world cultures. Invite the world into your classroom with this educational and exciting exploration!

1. Give students a copy of the **Capitals for the Capitals reproducible (page 38)**.

2. Have students match the names of the capital cities with the correct set of configuration boxes by looking for tall and short letters that fit. Configuration boxes help children recognize the size and space needed for each letter when writing. Have them rewrite the name of each capital in the boxes using correct capitalization. Emphasize that names of people and places begin with a capital letter.

3. Help them sound out each syllable to say the city and country names aloud. Then point out the location of each country and city on a world map.

4. Pair up students with partners from an older grade, teacher's helpers, or parent volunteers. Assign each pair a capital city to locate on a world map or atlas (include other cities such as Paris, Ottawa, Jerusalem, Mexico City, Beijing, and Washington, DC). Ask students to find two interesting facts about their city using classroom resources, and write them on sentence strips.

5. Invite pairs to draw a picture illustrating something about this city or country. They can also use magazines, computer clip art, and so on.

6. Display all sentence strips and illustrations in a Class World Gallery. Invite other classes to come and "tour the world" in your classroom. Invite parent volunteers to bring in different cultural foods, share family photos, and play multicultural music for the celebration!

Paris has a famous art museum called the Louvre

The Eiffel Tower is in Paris.

Inclusion Tip

Show students videos of different countries to highlight cultural elements, while capitalizing on auditory and visual modalities.

Capitals for the Capitals

Directions: Look at the letter boxes. Some are for tall letters, and some are for short letters. Can you match each set of boxes with a capital city? Write the correct capital city in each set of boxes.

| Lima | London | Canberra | Tokyo |

1.

2.

3.

4.

CHAPTER 3

Mathematics

Math is vital for developing critical thinking skills across the curriculum. Math is not just adding and subtracting; it also includes conceptual lessons such as estimating, visualizing, deducing, and recognizing patterns. Math helps students in everyday, real-life situations such as averaging test scores, shopping, making change, telling time, measuring, and more.

Classroom Counting

Counting begins by associating numbers with objects. Numbers do not exist in a vacuum; they represent quantities. Math becomes truly useful when it is applied to the real world.

Give students a copy of the **Classroom Counting reproducible (page 40)**. Invite them to work individually or in pairs to find and count each item in the classroom scene. Have students write the corresponding letter over each item to help them keep count. For example, *pencils–A, books–B, windows–C*. Then have students go back and count how many letters are the same and write the number in their charts. Later, provide real classroom items for students to count (e.g., pencils, desks, crayons, desks). Have students work in teams to count and tally each group of items.

Happy Math

Some students can feel intimated by math. This fear can trigger negative feelings and ultimately a strong dislike of the subject. Positive subliminal messages that say "math is fun" can help change students' attitudes. Achieve positive associations by using smiling faces! **Use the Happy Math reproducible (page 41)** to teach students skills in counting, skip-counting, and, of course, a positive math attitude!

Inclusion Tip

Allow students to refer to a 100s chart, number line, or ruler to help them recognize part–whole relationships, patterns, and missing elements.

Name _____ Date _____

Classroom Counting

Directions: Count each object listed below. Write the letter over each object in the picture. Then count all the letters. Write the number in the chart.

pencil – A	books – B	desks – C
flags – D	computers – E	crayons – F

Object	How Many?	Object	How Many?
pencils		crayons	
books		flags	
desks		computers	

Reproducible   978-1-4129-5233-0 • © Corwin Press

Happy Math

Directions: Count the number of happy faces in each row. How many should be in the empty box? Draw the correct number of happy faces in each empty box to finish the row.

1.

| 😊 | 😊 😊 | | 😊 😊
😊 😊 |

2.

| 😊 😊
😊 😊 | | 😊 😊 😊
😊 😊 😊 | 😊 😊 😊 😊
😊 😊 😊 😊 |

3.

| 😊 😊 | 😊 😊
😊 😊 | | 😊 😊 😊 😊
😊 😊 😊 😊 |

4.

| 😊 😊 😊 | | 😊 😊 😊
😊 😊 😊
😊 😊 😊 | 😊 😊 😊 😊
😊 😊 😊 😊
😊 😊 😊 😊 |

5.

| | 😊 😊 😊 | 😊 😊 | 😊 |

6.

| 😊 😊 😊 😊
😊 😊 😊 😊 | 😊 😊 😊
😊 😊 😊 | | 😊 😊 |

Counting on the Farm

There is more than one way to record answers for math problems. This fun counting activity shows students that numbers are not the only way to show answers. They can show numbers with words, tally marks, numerals, and even objects such as farm animals! Give students a copy of the **Counting on the Farm reproducible (page 43)**. Have them count each group of items and animals, and then cross out the item that doesn't belong.

Inclusion Tip

Ask students to verbalize their choices—numerals, objects, words, or tally marks. Have them block out other problems with a sheet of paper so they can concentrate on one at a time.

Edible Estimations

Estimation is an important math skill for students to develop at an early age. They will use this skill throughout their lives, almost every day. This activity provides an entertaining and easy introduction to making estimates. Note: Before doing this activity, make sure to check students' health records to see if they have any food allergies or diet restrictions.

1. Give each student a copy of the **Edible Estimates reproducible (page 44)** and a bag of jellybeans, M&M's®, or other small manipulatives.

2. Invite students to guess, or estimate, how many items will fit in each circle. Have them write their guess under each circle.

3. Have students put the items in the circles and count the actual number. Then have them write the actual number. Encourage them to note the difference between the two numbers.

4. Afterward, invite students to share and compare their estimates. They can also create bar graphs and patterns using different colored items.

Inclusion Tip

Have students work in pairs. One can place candies while the other counts. One can write the answers while the other notes the difference between guesses and actual numbers.

978-1-4129-5233-0

Counting on the Farm

Directions: Count the animals and tally marks in each row. Look at the words and numbers. Draw an X on the item in each row that does not belong.

1.

five　　　5

2.

3　　　three

3.

eight  　　　ate

4.

7

5.

one　　　1　　　won

6.

four 　　　4

Edible Estimates

Directions: Follow these steps:

1. Guess how many items will fit in each circle. Write your guess in the chart.

2. Place items in each circle until no more will fit.

3. Count the items in each circle. Write the number in the chart.

Guess: _____   Actual: _____

Guess: _____

Actual: _____

Guess: _____

Actual: _____

Unifix® Cubes

Unifix® cubes and rods are great for teaching number value, place value, counting, and number order. All students can benefit from visualizing this "mathematical staircase." Unifix® cubes can help students perform math operations such as addition, subtraction, multiplication, and division with whole numbers and fractions.

Inclusion Tip

Students with greater cognitive needs can trace or fill in the cube outline with the rods or Unifix® cubes.

Give students a copy of the **Math Cubes reproducible (page 46)**. Students can use these cubes to help them solve the problems. If you have Unifix® cubes or other counters, allow students to manipulate them when solving math problems.

Money Matters

Money is one of those real-world skills students should learn at a young age. They learn how to identify coins and small bills, their values, how those values compare to one another. Understanding money at an early age sets an excellent foundation for later learning with percents, decimals, and fractions.

Give students a copy of the **Money Matters reproducible (page 47)**. Invite them to work individually or in pairs to answer the questions. Allow students to use coins or manipulatives to help complete the task.

Inclusion Tip

More advanced learners can do more difficult money-counting activities, while some learners might only identify or sort different types of coins.

Math Cubes

Directions: Use the cubes to help you add and subtract.

1. 5 − 3 = _____
         T

2. 4 + 3 = _____
         A

3. 6 − 1 = _____
         I

4. 2 + 7 = _____
         F

5. 3 + 1 = _____
         M

6. 4 + 6 = _____
         H

7. 5 − 5 = _____
         U

8. 9 − 1 = _____
         S

9. 6 − 3 = _____
         N

Can you solve the puzzle?

Write the letter on the line with the matching answer. It tells a secret message!

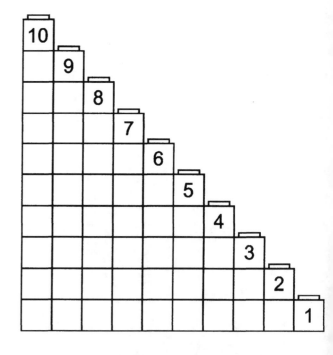

___ ___ ___ ___   ___ ___   ___ ___ ___
 4   7   2   10   5   8   9   0   3

Name _____ Date _____

Money Matters

Directions: Use these coin values to answer the questions.

1. How many = ? _____

2. How many = ? _____

3. How many =  ? _____

4. How many = ? _____

5. How many =  ? _____

6. How many =  ? _____

7. How many =   ? _____

100s Chart

A 100s chart is an invaluable tool for helping children learn number order, patterns, addition, subtraction, skip-counting, and more. To include a tactile and visual element, students can place their fingers or counters on numbers and/or highlight numbers as they listen to oral counting, follow written directions, and identify number patterns. They can go backward to subtract, forward to add, and even highlight multiples to learn about multiplication. The possibilities are endless!

Give students a copy of the **100s Chart** and **From 1 to 100 reproducibles (pages 49 and 50)**. Invite them to use the 100s Chart to complete the From 1 to 100 worksheet. When they are done, students can save their 100s Chart in a math folder to use for future math activities.

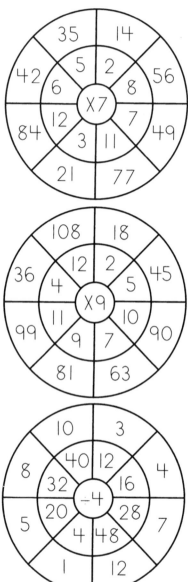

Inclusion Tip

On the computer, create blank 10 x 10 tables for students to fill in missing numbers. Begin by omitting *1–10*, then *1–20*, *1–30*, multiples of two, three, four, and so on, with increasing difficulty. Be certain that students fill in numbers from left to right.

Math Wheels

In order to be successful mathematicians, students must have command of basic addition, subtraction, multiplication, and division facts. That means being able to respond to facts quickly using "mental math." The **Math Wheels reproducible (page 51)** can be used repeatedly by varying the sign and numbers to teach and reinforce basic math skills. On the left side of the page are some samples of math wheels you can create for your students to solve.

Inclusion Tip

To add an interpersonal component, pair up students to cooperatively solve problems. One student can be the "computer," and one, using a calculator, can be the "checker."

Name _____ Date _____

100s Chart

Name _____ Date _____

From 1 to 100

Directions : Write the number that comes before and after each number below.

_____   _____
- - - - - - -   - - - - - - -
_____ 15 _____
_____   _____
- - - - - - -   - - - - - - -
_____ 39 _____
_____   _____
- - - - - - -   - - - - - - -
_____ 81 _____

Directions: Find the correct numbers. Use your 100s Chart.

1. Write the odd numbers from 1 to 20.

_____

- -

_____

2. Write the even numbers from 50 to 70.

_____

- -

_____

Name _____ Date _____

Math Wheels

Directions: Use your 100s Chart to help you.

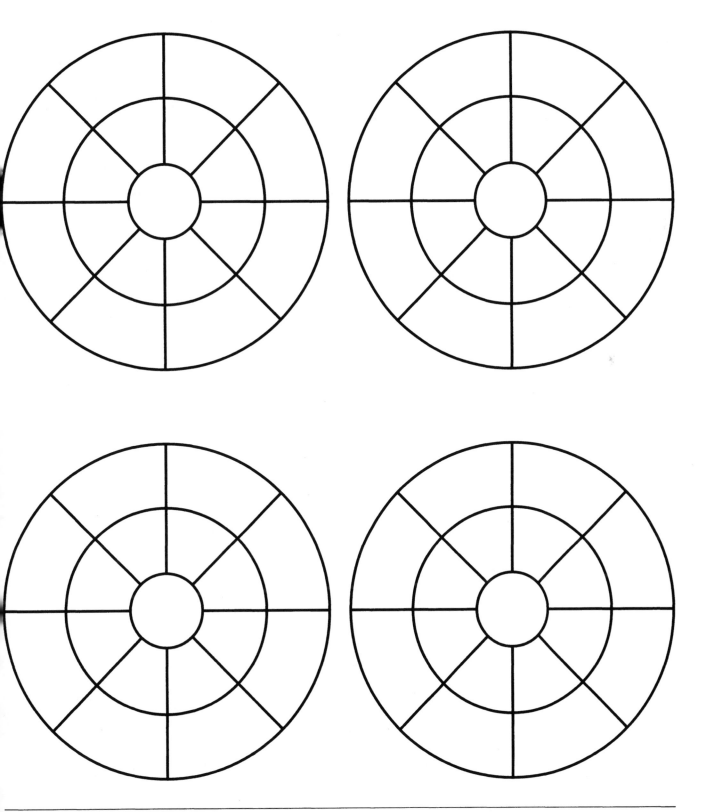

On the Clock

Time is a constant in our world. It surrounds us in words, numbers, appointments, school activities, television shows, and just about every aspect of our lives. Telling and managing time can be a challenging task for young learners. Digital clocks are good for a quick check on the time but they do not teach the whole picture. Students need to understand where they fit into the concepts of past, present, and future.

Give students a copy of the **Time Flies reproducible (page 53)**. They will not only learn how to tell time, but also recognize how time figures into their daily lives.

Inclusion Tip

Conduct sporadic classroom time checks, asking students to identify the time of day. Record answers on the board next to a name or an activity picture. This adds a visual component to match the time with the event.

Learning with Shapes

Students can learn about shapes in a variety of ways. However, differing abilities can affect the way students approach this task. You might ask students to simply name or trace shapes, count and measure shapes' sides, or recognize shapes in the classroom.

Give students pictures of simple shapes such as squares, circles, rectangles, and triangles. Then give the following directions:

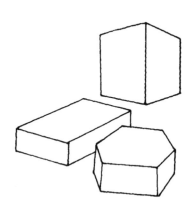

1. Name the shape.

2. Trace the shape.

3. Count the number of sides on each shape.

4. Use toothpicks to form each shape.

5. Use a ruler to measure the sides of each shape.

6. Look around the classroom. List objects with similar shapes.

Inclusion Tip

Allow kinesthetic learners to manipulate 3-D foam, plastic, or wooden shapes.

Build interpersonal skills by having the class create a shape bulletin board of real-world objects, such as a rectangular school bus, a triangular ice cream cone, and so on.

Go on a "shape walk" around the schoolyard, asking students to point out recognizable shapes.

Time Flies

Directions: Look at the time on each clock. Do you go to school before or after each time? Circle **Before** or **After**.

I go to school...

Before   After

Before   After

Before   After

Before   After

Before   After

Before   After

CHAPTER 4

Connecting Students to the Curriculum

Although specific standards must be met in each grade, teachers should first reach students on a level they can understand and form relationships. Subjects such as math, science, reading, art, music, physical education, and social studies can be connected to each other and tied to students' lives in meaningful ways. Teaching primary students how to relate to concepts across the curriculum plants seeds for important adult skills such as multi-tasking, thinking analytically, and applying learning to a multitude of events and situations.

My Favorite Things

Begin your school year with an interest inventory to find out more about students' individual likes and dislikes. Give students a copy of the **My Favorite Things reproducible (page 55)** on the first day of school. After they have filled out the page, collect and file the pages for future reference. At the end of the school year, ask students to fill out the reproducible again to see if their choices stayed the same or changed.

Refer to students' choices in order to infuse their interests into the curriculum. For example, for a unit on changes in nature, ask students to identify their favorite season and the changes that take place during that season. Activities such as these motivate students, personalize the learning, and increase understanding.

Inclusion Tip

Concrete learners and those with emerging literacy skills may have to dictate their thoughts to a classmate or teacher helper. As another option, students can cut out pictures from magazines or tie in technology with computer clip art.

Name _____   Date _____

My Favorite Things

Directions: Draw a picture or write a few words inside each box to tell about your favorite things. Share your ideas with your classmates.

Food	Book	Movie
TV Show	Pet	Game/Sport
Song	Subject	Hobby

Favorite Seasons Bar Graph

Promote group cooperation and interpersonal skills by having students work together to create bar graphs. This activity incorporates the multiple intelligences in a variety of ways—visual-spatial, mathematical-logical, bodily-kinesthetic, and verbal-linguistic.

For this activity, you will need the following materials:

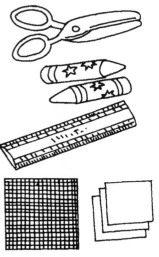

- students' completed My Favorite Things reproducibles

- writing paper

- colored construction paper squares

- crayons or markers

- rulers

- scissors

- glue

- large-sized graph paper

1. Ahead of time, draw a four-grid box on drawing paper. Label the separate boxes *Fall, Winter, Spring*, and *Summer*. Make a copy of the grid for each student.

2. Divide the class into four groups, one for each season. If possible, group together students who like the same season.

3. Read aloud students' favorite season responses from their My Favorite Things reproducibles. As each season is announced, have students make a tally mark in the corresponding season box of their grids.

4. When you're finished reading the responses, have students add the totals. If needed, model this step on the board or an overhead projector to reinforce visual learning.

5. Model for students how to make a simple bar graph. Use different colored construction paper squares to show the result for each season. Demonstrate how to make a key to show which color represents which season.

6. After modeling, invite each group to make their own bar graphs. Walk around the room to help students as they work.

7. When students are finished with their graphs, invite groups to work together to write three to five sentences on writing paper to

explain why they like that season best. Have them glue or tape this paper to their graph.

8. Bring the class together again. Then invite individual students in each group to act out different activities people like to do during their assigned season. Ask the class to guess each activity.

9. Interest inventories can be used again and again to encourage peer interaction and cooperative writing exercises that connect learners with various subjects and each other (e.g., favorite movies, pets, books, subjects, and more).

Inclusion Tip

Help students understand the concepts of horizontal and vertical by standing up and demonstrating with their arms. You can also invite a volunteer to stand while another lies down on a classroom rug.

Different Ways of Learning

Saying that students learn differently within the multiple intelligences is really just another way of saying that each student is unique! Self-awareness of likes and dislikes is important for young learners. You should also be aware of your own preferred (stronger) and weaker intelligences. If you do not like a subject, you might subliminally send out negative messages to students, such as *I don't like or feel comfortable with this topic.* All intelligences and students have value!

Give students a copy of the **Ways of Learning reproducible (page 59)**. Invite them to look at the pictures and think about which activities they like best and least. Help students rank the activities by writing the numbers *1–9* in the boxes. Prompt them with questions such as: *Which activity do you like best? Which activity do you like second best? Which is your least favorite activity?*

The multiple intelligences are labeled as follows:

1. Verbal/Linguistic—Book Smart

2. Interpersonal—People Smart

3. Bodily/Kinesthetic—Body Smart

4. Visual/Spatial—Picture Smart

5. Logical/Mathematical—Number Smart

6. Naturalistic—Nature Smart

7. Intrapersonal—Self Smart

8. Musical/Rhythmic—Music Smart

9. Existential—Infinite/Philosophy Smart (Beyond What You See)

Inclusion Tip

Encourage and praise students who attempt activities outside of their favorite intelligence. Remind them to be kind to themselves and others as they attempt new activities. In other words, it's more important to enjoy playing a sport than to be the star athlete!

Name _____ Date _____

Ways of Learning

Directions: Listen to your teacher for directions.

Book Smart	People Smart	Body Smart
Picture Smart	Self Smart	Number Smart
Nature Smart	Music Smart	Question Smart

Rules of Conversation

Students can develop proper conversational skills at an early age. Use a simple rule such as "one person speaks at a time while others listen." This lesson connects speaking and listening skills with topics across the curriculum. Invite students to choose a different topic to discuss each week. (Cover a variety of topics from across the curriculum, including those from daily lessons.)

1. Ahead of time, make several copies of the **Speaking and Listening reproducible (page 61)**. Make sure you have one ear for each student and one mouth for the speaker. Cut out and laminate each picture and glue it to a craft stick.

2. Gather students into a circle, and tell them you are going to practice speaking and listening skills. Provide several topics for students to choose from. Distribute an ear card to each student.

3. Hold up the mouth card, and tell students they are going to discuss the topic one at a time. They will hold up their ear cards while they are listening to the speaker. Explain that only one person speaks at a time and that they should listen carefully by looking at the speaker and sitting still. When the speaker is finished, he or she gives the mouth card to another student, who then takes a turn speaking.

4. Give the mouth card to a student in the circle, inviting him or her to speak about the topic. When this student is finished, he or she hands the mouth card to another student, and so on. Continue until all students have had a chance to speak.

Inclusion Tip

If students have attention issues or are fidgety, allow them to stand instead of sit or do some stretching exercises. Use a private signal with some students to indicate *Yes, you are on task,* or *Uh-oh, you are treading on thin ice!*

978-1-4129-5233-0

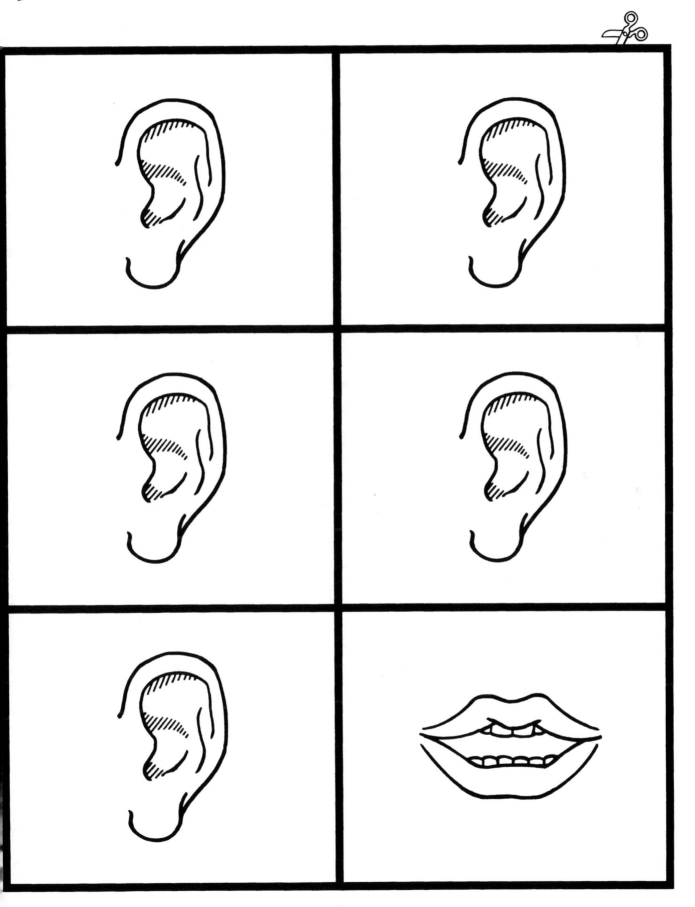

Our Emotions

Visuals can aid learning in a profound and concrete way. Giving students visuals helps them to connect what they see to what they hear and connect pictures to ideas and feelings. In this activity, you will read aloud one or more of the following books about emotions and feelings (e.g., grumpy, happy, angry, nervous, sad). Students then use pictures to connect first to the characters' feelings and then to their own.

1. Give students a copy of the **Feelings Faces reproducible (page 63)**. Tell them to cut out each face. From the list below, choose one of the books to read aloud.

2. As you read, encourage students to think about the feelings and emotions described in the book. Pause at appropriate times to ask questions such as: *What do you think this character is feeling right now?* Tell students to hold up the face showing the character's emotions.

3. When you are finished reading, ask students to think about the emotions described in the book. Discuss with students when they might have felt these same emotions. Invite volunteers to share a time they felt sad, angry, happy, anxious, and so on.

Books About Feelings/Emotions

Alexander and the Terrible, Horrible, No Good, Very Bad Day
by Judith Viorst
The Grouchy Ladybug by Eric Carle
How Are You Peeling? Foods with Moods
by Saxton Freyman and Joost Elffers
The Mixed-Up Chameleon
by Eric Carle
The Mixed-Up Morning
by Mercer Mayer
The Very Lonely Firefly by Eric Carle
The Very Quiet Cricket by Eric Carle
Where's Your Smile, Crocodile?
by Claire Freedman

Inclusion Tip

Praise students with behavioral issues who share appropriate emotions. Reinforce the fact that there are no "good" or "bad" emotions, just individual expressions, choices, and reactions. However, these choices should never harm oneself or others.

Name _____ Date _____

Feelings Faces

✂

Sad

Happy

Scared

Surprised

Grumpy

Angry

Excited

Confused

Me in the Universe

Sometimes, students need help understanding their place in their neighborhood, community, city, state, country, and the world as a whole. These abstract concepts can be difficult for young learners to grasp. Primary grade students often think that the world begins with them. This concrete activity can help to change that way of thinking.

1. Give students a copy of the **Me in the Universe reproducible (page 65)**. Tell them that this activity is going to help them find their place in the universe. Have students cut apart the word cards. (If the words are too difficult to read, break them up into syllables.)

2. Direct students to work with a partner to put the words or ideas in order from smallest to largest. The objective for some students is to simply recognize size order, understanding the "me" card as the smallest part of the universe.

3. When students are finished ordering their cards, tell them to write 1 on the card with the smallest item, 2 for the next biggest item, and so on, until they reach 9.

4. Discuss students' results as a whole class. Use a large class world map and other visuals to help students "see" the concepts.

Inclusion Tip

To make a kinesthetic connection, ask students to hold two hands together for *me*. Then have them separate their hands more and more for *family*, *community*, *city*, *state*, and so on, until their hands are farthest apart for *universe*.

Me in the Universe

Me	Family	Community

City	State	Country

Continent	World	Universe
		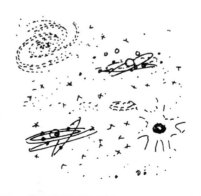

CHAPTER 5

Comprehension and Study Skills

The time students spend in school is only the beginning of learning. Educators will acknowledge that the students who do best in class are those who also complete homework assignments on time and review learned concepts at home. It is important to instill these good study habits in young learners while encouraging the home-to-school connection.

Setting Learning Goals

Setting goals for learning is the first step in creating a foundation for good study habits. This activity will encourage students to think about how they approach learning and how to develop good study habits. Give each student several copies of the **My Learning Goals reproducible (page 67)**. Go over each statement with the class and discuss the different strategies students can use to approach and learn new concepts and then reflect on their study habits.

To get started, help each student set one or two personal goals for learning or studying a specific topic (e.g., addition facts, spelling, reading). Then ask students to use their charts to help them achieve those goals. Each day, they will write *Y* for *yes*, *N* for *no*, or *S* for *sometimes* in the chart to show what they did that week to meet their goals.

Encourage students to continue to set learning goals throughout the year and keep track of what they do each week to achieve these goals.

Inclusion Tip

Students with cognitive and behavioral issues may need more frequent, intermittent monitoring to ensure long-term goals are achieved. Happy faces, praise, smiles, and instruction on positive self-talk goes a long way! Parent-teacher communication is also recommended.

Name _____ Date _____

My Learning Goals

Directions: Write **Y** for Yes, **N** for No, or **S** for Sometimes.

_____

- -

My Learning Goal: _____

	Monday	Tuesday	Wednesday	Thursday	Friday
I read about it.					
I heard about it.					
I asked questions.					
I practiced in class.					
I reviewed it at home.					
I did my homework.					
I learned it!					

Daily Behavior Chart

A daily behavior chart is a good strategy for making students aware of their behavior. The chart below can be used again and again to reinforce and check behavior with students, one on one. It is deliberately small so that other classmates can't see it. It is meant as concrete reinforcement between you and each student.

Make one copy of the chart below for each student, and glue it to an index card. Keep all cards in a file box at your desk. Throughout the day, you can check off or initial appropriate ratings for each time slot or day, and then help the student total daily points. Although this might be difficult to implement in a busy classroom, the time spent is well worth it! Younger students with social and or attention issues really benefit from this type of concrete structure and reinforcement to improve behavior. By making them more aware of their own patterns and choices, they'll begin to realize how visible their behavior is and how it affects others around them.

Inclusion Tip

Inform parents of students' daily behavior by establishing a structured school-home communication (e.g., weekly e-mails, phone calls, and/or charts) to encourage behavioral consistencies in both environments.

Time/Day	Great Job! 3 points	Good Choice! 2 points	I need reminding. 1 points	I can do much better! 0 points

Adapted from A Visual Tool for Early or Concrete Learners Source: Karten, T. (2005) *Inclusion Strategies That Work!* Thousand Oaks, CA: Corwin Press.

earning in the Right Direction

Many educators agree that many young learners, especially those with attention deficit issues, have a difficult time comprehending new concepts and ideas. This simple activity gives fidgety learners an acceptable reason to move around. In addition, it teaches map and listening skills!

Place large arrows (like those on a compass rose) on the chalkboard or white board, and point to specific directions, such as north, south, east, and west. To simplify, you can call the arrows up, down, left, and right. For more complexity, you can add southwest, southeast, northeast, and northwest.

Ask students to stand up. Then name different directions, one at a time. Ask students to point their arms in the matching direction. As students progress, you can instruct them to point or say the opposite direction. When students sit down, notice how much more attentive they become!

Use this activity during longer periods of sitting. As a variation, students can improve eye coordination by following a flashlight pointing in different directions. If this is physically taxing for a student, he or she can be the "compass coach" or "light keeper."

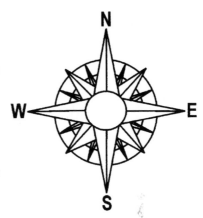

Learning Boxes

Neatly packaged learning is easier for young students to comprehend. Learning boxes are a great way for students to package, or compartmentalize, new concepts and ideas. Eventually, these "learning boxes" become internalized, as the brain no longer needs to see these concrete separations.

Give each student several copies of the **Learning Boxes reproducible (page 70)** to keep in a folder. After a specific lesson is taught or you are reviewing a concept, invite students to draw pictures or write words or phrases to show or describe what they learned. Learning boxes can be used across subject areas and are perfect for reviewing concepts and ideas throughout the school year.

Inclusion Tip

Form cooperative study groups who review each other's learning boxes while you reaffirm concepts and correct any misunderstandings.

Name _____ Date _____

Learning Boxes

Directions: What did you learn today? Draw pictures in the boxes and write words on the lines.

Subject

☐

_____

- - - - - - - - - - - - - -

_____

_____

- - - - - - - - - - - - - -

_____

Subject

☐

_____

- - - - - - - - - - - - - -

_____

_____

- - - - - - - - - - - - - -

_____

Subject

☐

_____

- - - - - - - - - - - - - -

_____

_____

- - - - - - - - - - - - - -

_____

Different Ways of Communicating

Some students are unable to respond to questions verbally due to speech issues, cognitive levels, or emotional factors. Quite often, students with special needs have better receptive than expressive language. Therefore, it's important to provide students with different ways to communicate.

The **Pick a Picture** and **Look, Listen, Think! reproducibles (pages 72 and 73)** provide simple, alternate methods for communication. The Pick a Picture activity allows students to respond to pictures and ideas by pointing or using counters. The Look, Listen, Think! activity allows students to respond by drawing. Pictures are worth a thousand words!

For the Pick a Picture activity, read the following directions to students. Direct them to respond by pointing or placing counters on their answers.

1. Point to the things you like to do.

2. Point to something that scares you.

3. Point to something that you eat.

4. Point to a place.

5. Point to a person.

6. Point to something whose name begins with the letter *m*.

7. Point to an animal you like.

8. Point to a picture that makes you smile a lot.

Categories: Living and Nonliving

Categorizing ideas with pictures and simple words yields faster retention and increased understanding. Students will learn to picture the abstract.

Give students a copy of the **Living or Nonliving reproducible (page 72)**. Tell them to cut apart the picture cards. Then have students work individually or with a partner to sort the cards into two categories–*living* and *nonliving*. Challenge students with questions about their groupings, such as: *Can you name two nonliving things that were made from something living?*

Inclusion Tip

More advanced students can divide the living and nonliving items into additional categories (e.g., animal; plant; similar shape, size, and color).

Name _____ Date _____

Pick a Picture

Directions: Point to the picture to answer your teacher's question.

Name _____ Date _____

Look, Listen, Think!

Directions: Read each sentence and look at the picture.
Put an X in the box if the student is doing the right thing.

1. Look at the teacher when he or she is talking.

2. Listen to the words the teacher is saying.

3. Erase other things from your mind.

4. Think about right now.

5. Ask questions if you do not get it!

Directions: Draw a picture of yourself listening in class on the back of this paper.

Name _____ Date _____

Living or Nonliving

Visualization

Visualizing concepts is a rather abstract task for younger, more concrete learners. They often need the concept demonstrated concretely or accompanied by an illustration. Visualization helps concepts "jump off the page" into students' minds. This skill will help students as they move forward into the upper grades. Here are a few examples from across the curriculum.

Inclusion Tip

Block out noise and distractions by placing cut-up tennis balls under chair legs, and lowering the lights and shades to reduce glare.

Students with visual impairments can think about what they might *hear* in different environments (e.g., animal and letter sounds). Responses can be verbalized, sung, pantomimed, or drawn.

Language Arts
Picture these things that begin with the letter B: bed, boy, butter, baby. Can you see them? What letter do you see next to each object?

Science
Pretend you are a fish swimming in the ocean. What kinds of plants and animals do you see?

Math
Imagine you won two stuffed animals at the carnival. Then your friend won three. How many stuffed animals do the two of you have all together?

Social Studies
Picture your neighborhood stores. What are they selling? What would you like to buy?

CHAPTER 6

Reflective Assessment, Testing, and Grading

Before considering alternate assessments, look carefully at the general education curriculum requirements. In the past, learners with special needs were often removed from mainstream learning and placed in separate classes with lower requirements. Unfortunately, this resulted in many adults being ill prepared to meet societal demands.

Assessments take many shapes and forms. Grades can be obtained from portfolios, observations, tests and quizzes, homework, reports, class projects and participation, and more. Students with special needs often do not fare well with typical assessments. Reasons for failure can vary from lower cognitive levels, poor or inappropriate instruction, and sometimes a lack of motivation and/or attention.

This situation calls for both you and the student to challenge your way of thinking. Ask yourself: *Is there another way I can teach this subject to this student?* Students should ask themselves: *Have I tried my best?* Both teachers and students should be involved in the assessment process.

My Progress Chart

Increase student responsibility by asking them to get involved with their own assessment! The **My Progress Chart reproducible (page 77)** provides students with that opportunity. Tell students they will use the chart to assess their own progress and achievements throughout the year. This primary rubric can be used for homework, class projects, group assignments, class discussions, and more. The ultimate goal is to increase student accountability and responsibility.

Inclusion Tip

If vertical adding is too difficult, concrete learners can write the correct number of tally marks in each box and then add them up.

Name _____   Date _____

My Progress Chart

Directions: Circle one statement in each row.
Then add up your points.

Excellent! (4 points)	Very Good! (3 points)	Good! (2 points)	I Can Do Better (1 point)	Poor
I did all of my work on time.	I did most of my work.	I did more than half of my work.	I did less than half of my work.	I did not do any of my work.
I tried my very best!	I tried hard.	I tried sometimes.	I did not try very hard.	I did not try at all.
I ask and answer questions all the time.	I ask and answer a lot of questions.	I ask and answer some questions.	I ask and answer a few questions.	I do not ask or answer any questions.
I always share with and help others	I share with and help others a lot.	I sometimes share with and help others.	I share with and help others a little bit.	I never share with or help others.
Total:	Total:	Total:	Total:	Total:

0 1 2 3 4 5 6 7 8 9 10 11 12 13 14 15 16

Lowest Score   **Highest Score**

Award Certificates

Everyone likes knowing that he or she did a great job. It means a lot to students when they get that extra special pat on the back for completing an assignment on time, trying hard at a task, helping another student, or learning a new concept. Acknowledging students' efforts will give them the pride and self-confidence to keep moving forward and conquering new challenges. There's an adage that says, "Success breeds success!" Early learners can be nourished with extra smiles, small prizes like stickers or pencils, or special certificates.

Make several copies of the **Award Certificates reproducible (page 79)** on colored card stock. Whenever you catch a student accomplishing a task, putting out extra effort, or helping another student, give him or her one of these certificates. It's just one more way of recognizing a great job! Additional ways to use the Award Certificates include:

- Make a bulletin board titled *Our Class Does a Great Job!* Whenever a student gets a certificate, post it on the bulletin board for the whole class to see!

- Keep some certificates in a decorated box on your desk. Invite students to give certificates to each other when they see a classmate doing something special.

- Send certificates home with students so families can share in the pride and post them on the refrigerator.

Inclusion Tip
Celebrate the abilities of all students, and honor everyone's strengths!

978-1-4129-5233-0

Great Job!

put out extra special efforts today.
You are a star student!

Super Helper!

We love how

helped others today.
You are the best!

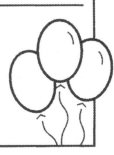

Show What You Know!

Enough of paper and pencil tests! There are many other ways students can show what they know. Diversity in testing practices embraces the multiple intelligences as well as student individualities and challenges. To accommodate student differences, offer a variety of ways for students to show you what they've learned. Tasks can be completed independently or cooperatively, but students must relate them to the topic. This open-ended approach acknowledges individual abilities and talents. For example, if students are responding to questions about the weather, they can list words or sing a song about rainy, sunny, and cloudy days.

Photocopy and enlarge the **Show What You Know! reproducible (page 81)**. Post the chart in an accessible place in the classroom. Whenever students are being tested on a certain topic, invite them to point to their choice on the chart.

Multiple Choices

Students will run across many multiple-choice tests throughout their academic careers. Learning how to approach these kinds of tests is an essential skill. The **Multiple Choice reproducible (page 82)** offers students preliminary practice in answering multiple-choice questions. Some choices are related to the questions, but they do not answer it correctly. Other choices do not relate to the question at all. Early learners need practice in critical thinking skills to eliminate ridiculous choices as well as tricky ones.

Provide students with the following multiple-choice tips:

- Read the question completely and carefully.

- Look at or read each answer before making your choice.

- Get rid of answers you know are wrong first.

- If you don't know the answer, move on to the next question and come back to it later.

Inclusion Tip

Encourage students with visual/perceptual, concentration, and/or learning differences to focus on question at a time and cover other distracting text with a folded sheet of paper.

Show What You Know!

Talk about it.	Make a list.	Act it about.
Sing a song.	Do a dance.	Use the computer.
Draw a picture.	Tell a joke.	Teach it.

Multiple Choice

Directions: Circle the correct picture to answer each question.

Com-mu-ni-ca-tion

1. Circle something that helps you talk to people far away.

2. Circle something that you send in the mail.

Trans-por-ta-tion

3. Circle something that helps you travel on water.

4. Circle something that helps you travel in the air.

 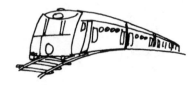 

Creating a Climate for Classroom Acceptance

Even if you have minimal experience instructing students with exceptionalities, you can still achieve successful inclusion for all students! First, establish a level of comfort and trust amongst you, the students, and their parents. Second, increase your knowledge of cognitive, behavioral, sensory, communication, physical, and learning differences through simulations, literature, and daily academic and social interactions. Most important, maintain a positive mindset, which most often yields positive and beneficial inclusion results.

Accepting others should come naturally to all of us. In today's inclusive classrooms, students need help realizing that there are differences amongst all of us. These are the very things that make us special and unique! Through early training, students can learn to accept people as they really are and maximize the potential of who they can be. A positive classroom climate will create an atmosphere of acceptance where all individuals are valued!

How Can I Help?

Students may not have a peer with a disability in their classroom, yet that's all the more reason why sensitivity and exposure to differences and modeling proper behavior is essential. The goal is for students to think beyond themselves and develop into more caring, responsible individuals as both children and adults.

Use the **How Can I Help? reproducible (page 84)** to initiate discussion on how students can help others with differences or special needs. Have students complete the reproducible in small groups or individually. Then bring students together for a whole class discussion. If you have students with special needs in your class, be sensitive to how they might feel about certain parts of the discussion, particularly if they are singled out. Encourage students to offer ideas for appropriate ways they can help or behave. Guide them to realize that people with differences have the same wishes, desires, emotions, and intelligence as everyone else!

Inclusion Tip

Don't force relationships if students are not compatible. Respect individual choices, with or without disabilities. Focus on self-esteem and confidence-building activities. Students who feel good about themselves are less apt to put others down.

How Can I Help?

Directions: Think about ways you could help someone who is different.

How can I help . . .

1. A child who cannot see very well?

_____

- -

_____

2. A child who cannot hear very well?

_____

- -

_____

3. A child who cannot speak very well?

_____

- -

_____

4. A child who cannot move or walk very well?

_____

- -

_____

We All Have Value

Everyone is valuable, no matter what his or her differences and abilities. Every student has special skills and talents. Sometimes we just need to be reminded that differences make us the unique individuals we are. The following activities will help students see the value in each other's differences.

To complete these activities, you will need the following materials:

- 3 empty coffee cans
- money (one-dollar bill, 4 quarters, 100 pennies)
- empty opaque, plastic juice bottle
- paper lunch bag
- bag or box of rice

1. Place the following items in three separate coffee cans: one-dollar bill, 20 pennies, and one quarter. Shake each can individually, and ask students: *Which can do you think is worth more?* The lesson here is that sometimes, valuable things are not easy to identify. What we hear or see on the outside does not tell the whole story!

2. Place the following items in three separate coffee cans: one-dollar bill, 100 pennies, and four quarters. Shake each can individually, and ask students: *Which can do you think is worth more?* The lesson here is that we don't always know what's on the inside by what we see or hear on the outside. In this case, the cans are all equal, but in different ways. People are equal in different ways too!

3. Place equal amounts of rice in a coffee can, a juice bottle, and a lunch bag. Shake each container individually, and ask students: *What do you think is inside these containers?* The lesson here is that even though something appears different on the outside, the contents are the same. Every person has the same worth, regardless of what he or she looks like on the outside. Discuss the phrase *You can't judge a book by its cover*.

4. Ask students: *What do you think is worth more, rice or money?* Discuss the concept of *value* with students. Lead them to realize that rice would be worth more to a starving person on a deserted island. This person would have no use for money. The lesson here is that each person has different needs.

Books That Embrace Differences

The following books are great read-alouds for helping students increase their exposure and sensitivity to differing abilities. After reading a book, invite students to discuss the theme and concepts with a partner or in small cooperative groups. Students can draw pictures and discuss the characters, plot, and setting. Invite them to share what they learned in a kind and respectful way.

Apartment 3 by Ezra Jack Keats (blindness)

Be Good to Eddie Lee by Virginia Fleming (Down's Syndrome)

The Crayon Box That Talked by Shane DeRolf (appreciating differences)

Crow Boy by Taro Yashima (exclusion in schools)

Don't Call Me Special: A First Look at Disability by Pat Thomas (physical disabilities)

Eagle Eyes: A Child's Guide to Paying Attention by Jeanne Gehret (ADD/ADHD)

How Smudge Came by Nan Gregory (cognitive impairments)

I'm Like You, You're Like Me: A Child's Book About Understanding and Celebrating Each Other by Cindy Gainer (uniqueness and similarities)

Joey and Sam: A Heartwarming Storybook About Autism, a Family, and a Brother's Love by Illana Katz (autism)

Knots on a Counting Rope by Bill Martin Jr. and John Archambault (blindness)

Leo the Late Bloomer by Robert Kraus (abilities that bloom)

Luna and the Big Blur: A Story for Children Who Wear Glasses by Shirley Day (sight impairment)

Rolling Along with Goldilocks and the Three Bears by Cindy Meyers (physical disabilities)

Silent Lotus by Jean M. Lee (deafness)

The Sneetches by Dr. Seuss (differences)

Talk to Me by Sue Brearley (language disabilities)

What's Wrong with Timmy? by Maria Shriver (cognitive disabilities)

     978-1-4129-5233-0

Parent Survey

Student's Name: _____

Parent's/Guardian's Name: _____

1. What does my child think about school?

_____

2. What do I visualize my child doing in 10 or 15 years?

_____

3. What are my child's special or individual needs?

_____

4. Some words I would use to describe my child are:

_____

5. What are my child's favorite things to do?

_____

6. What would I change about my child's school or classroom experience?

_____

7. What do I like about my child's school or classroom?

_____

8. My areas of expertise that I could share with my child's class are:

_____

9. I'd like to volunteer to help with:

_____

10. You may contact me at:

_____

Home: _____ Work: _____ Cell: _____

E-mail: _____

Home Address: _____

_____

Charting Lessons

Use this chart to keep notes from IEPs you have read and monitor how lessons align with modifications and goals listed in the IEP.

Subject: _____   Teachers: _____

Modifications/Accommodations

MBHE—Modified, but high expectations   **C/T**—Computer/technology
G—Grading modified   **M**—Alternative materials
S—Seating   **OW**—Oral/written presentations
HW—Homework modified/reduced   **MS**—Multisensory techniques
P—Preteaching   **CST**—Child study team support
R—Reteaching/repetition   **PI**—Parental involvement
A—Assessment varied/simplified   **B**—Buddy system
SG—Study guide   **NT**—Note-taking system
V—Visuals   **LOV**—Learning objective varied
T—Extra time, or wait time for tasks   **O+**—Other modifications
BP—Behavior plan

Students	Modifications/ Accommodations	Assessments/Dates Mastery Level	Comments

ABCD Quarterly Checklist of Functional Objectives

Use these codes:

A = Always

B = Becoming better

C = Can do with reminders

D = Doesn't display behavior

Student Name: _____

OBJECTIVES	Q1	Q2	Q3	Q4
Establishes eye contact with teachers and peers				
Uses proper conversational tones				
Follows classroom and school rules				
Respects authority				
Exhibits social reciprocity				
Appropriately communicates needs				
Demonstrates consistent attention during classroom lessons				
Completes all classroom assignments				
Finishes all homework and long-range assignments				
Able to take class notes independently				
Writes legibly				
Keeps an organized work area				
Respects the property of others				
Works well with groups				
Adjusts to changes in routines				
Asks for clarification when needed				
Takes pride in achievements				
Displays enthusiasm about learning				

Student Referral Planner

WHY does this student need a referral? Is it for academic, behavioral, and/or social reasons? List the student's strengths and weaknesses on the reverse side of this planner.

WHO has been contacted? Is anyone currently seeing or supporting this child?

WHEN is a good time to observe this student?

WHAT strategies/implementations have you tried? Attach any documentation such as sample academic work, tests, or behavioral logs.

Student Referral Planner
(STOP and THINK)

HOW can the CST help?

WHERE is this student currently educated?

Curriculum Recording, Documentation, and Observations

Content Area: _____

Objectives: _____

_____

Student and/ or Dates	Student is able to fully participate in the same lesson as peers.	Student needs modified expectations and/or extra materials to accomplish lesson objectives.	Student can independently participate in a different but related assignment in the room.	Student cannot proficiently complete task in the classroom, even with support.	Brief comments, observations, needs, modifications, notes, V/A/K/T concerns, future plans

Classroom Structure to Promote Inclusion

Questions

- How can teachers teach the same topic while considering different levels of development and ability?

- What about classroom management?

- Can one teacher divide the class into focused groups?

In the classroom

- Everyone is learning together in one room.

- Different thought processes and levels (independent, instructional, frustrations) exist within the same room.

- Teaching everyone does not mean that students are learning the same breadth of material at the same time.

- The ultimate goal is progress for all based upon individual needs.

Lesson structure

Think of how your lessons are designed. Consider structuring your lessons as whole, part, whole. Stat as a whole group, break out into smaller groups and return to the whole group.

First, everyone in the class could	Whole

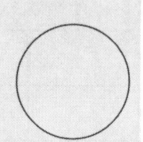

- Listen to the same story, poem, mathematical word problem

- Look at the same picture prompt related to the content

- Chorally read or write a story together on chart paper

- Have a group discussion about the topic

- Be introduced to science and social studies vocabulary

- Preview and discuss on what skill(s) the lesson will focus (e.g., scientific method, timelines, decimals, finding the main idea, how to improve writing by substituting words)

- Be involved in a teacher demonstration or experiment, handling concrete objects or lesson-related manipulatives

Second, students can work with smaller groups, partners, or individually to

Part

- Complete an assigned reading or writing task

- Create a product based upon what was learned (e.g., write a poem, story, or short skit; illustrate captioned pictures; solve a crossword puzzle, word search, or given problem; reenact an experiment; conduct research on the computer; read and learn more about the topic)

- Complete varying activities from a chapter, using matching colored paper (e.g. green, blue, yellow assignment) for better classroom management

- Complete learning tasks under teacher's auspices

During this time, walk around the classroom supervising or instructing smaller groups or individual students, while recording observations and individual needs evidenced.

Third, together the class becomes a whole unit again, while individual students, teachers, partners, and groups share

Whole
again

- What else they learned or discovered about the topic from a book, computer, other student, teacher, or self

- A finished product created

- What they now know, giving specific details

- What they still wonder about

- Questions about the material presented

This is basically a time for all learners to celebrate their discoveries and progress with each other, while validating and reflecting upon their own learning.

Three-Question Lesson Design

Lesson design requires asking these three simple questions:

1. What are you going to teach? ⟶ Objective

2. How are you going to teach it? ⟶ Procedure

3. Did it work? ⟶ Assessment

Special education can be special for everyone involved, if you consider the following factors. Remember, not every lesson requires all of these ingredients, but perhaps being cognizant of their importance will allow these objectives to evolutionarily diffuse into the repertoires of all teachers. Think about how the following points fit into your lessons:

- Topic

- Desired Goals (Social/Academic/Emotional/Physical/Cognitive)

- Baseline Knowledge

- Motivating Activity (Visual/Auditory/Kinesthetic-Tactile Sensory Elements)

- Critical/Creative Thinking Skills

- Interpersonal Activity/Cooperative Roles

- Curriculum Connections

- Possible Accommodations

- Parallel Activity

- Anticipated roles of General Educator/Special Educator/ Instructional Assistant/Student/Peers/Family/Specialists /Related Services

- Administration

- Adult/Peer/Self-Assessments

- Closure

- Revisitation Plans

Inclusive Reflections

Use this form to account for and take pride in both your own and your students' achievements and efforts. It's a speculative professional self-evaluation combined with an inclusive pedagogical student reflection. It shows where you and your students have been, where you are now, and where you are heading.

	YES	NO
Was this student's prior knowledge increased?		
Even though this student did not receive a passing grade (e.g., 50% on an evaluation), did he or she master 50% of the material?		
Do you think this student will be more proficient when he or she learns about this topic, content area, or skill again?		
Is there a way to repeat this learning and somehow individualize instruction within the classroom (e.g., alternate assignment on the same topic) if appropriate support is given, such as a parent, peer coach, or paraeducator?		
Would assigning a peer coach be beneficial to both this student and his or her student mentor?		
Can this student chart progress to take more ownership and responsibility for his or her learning?		
Is this student experiencing more accomplishments than frustrations with his or her inclusion experience in your class?		
Has physical inclusion allowed this student to develop a more positive self-image, which has translated to increased self-confidence and motivation?		
Are you experiencing personal and/or professional growth by having this student in your class?		

References

Armbruster, B., Lehr, F., & Osborn, J. *Put reading first: The research building blocks for teaching children to read: kindergarten through grade 3.* (2001). Retrieved May 9, 2006, from the National Institute for Literacy Web site: http://www.nifl.gov/partnershipforreading/publications/reading_first1.html#phonemic.

Harriott, W. (2004). *Inclusion inservice: Content and training procedures across the United States. Journal of Special Education Leadership, 17,* 91–102.

Karten, T. J. (2005). *Inclusion strategies that work! Research-based methods for the classroom.* Thousand Oaks, CA: Corwin Press.

McTighe, H., Seif, E., & Wiggins, G. (2004). *You can teach for meaning. Educational Leadership, 62,* 26–30.

National Council for the Social Studies. (2002). *Expectations of excellence: Curriculum standards for social studies.* Silver Spring, MD: National Council for the Social Studies (NCSS).

National Council of Teachers of English and International Reading Association. (1996). *Standards for the English language arts.* Urbana, IL: National Council of Teachers of English (NCTE).

National Council of Teachers of Mathematics. (2005). *Principles and standards for school mathematics.* Reston, VA: National Council of Teachers of Mathematics (NCTM).

National Research Council. (2005). *National science education standards.* Washington, DC: National Academy Press.

Nolet, V., & McLaughlin, M. (2005). *Accessing the general education curriculum: Including students with disabilities in standards-based reform.* Thousand Oaks, CA: Corwin Press.

Odom, S., Brantlinger, E., Gersten, R., Horner, R., Thompson, B., & Harris, K. (2005). *Research in special education: Scientific methods and evidence-based practices. Exceptional Children, 71,* 137–148.

Walsh, J., & Conner, T. (2004). *Increasing participation by students with disabilities in standards-based reform through teacher observations. Journal of Special Education Leadership, 17,* 103–110.

Yell, M., Katsiyanna, A., & Shiner, J. (2006). *Improving student services: The no child left behind act, adequate yearly progress, and students with disabilities. Teaching Exceptional Children, 38,* 32–39.

Young, S. (1994). *Scholastic rhyming dictionary.* New York: Scholastic Inc.

Zull, J. (2004). The art of changing the brain. *Educational Leadership, 62,* 68–72.

Printed in the United States
By Bookmasters